WORKBOOK

FOR

GREAT CEOS ARE LAZY
How Exceptional Ceos Do More in Less Time

[An Implementation Guide to Jim Schleckser's Book]

SARA PRESS

THIS BOOK BELONGS TO

_____

_____

_____

_____

_____

_____

This companion workbook is intended to be used as a supplement to the original book. It is not meant to replace the original book, but rather to enhance and deepen the understanding of the concepts presented in the original book.

TABLE OF CONTENTS

How To Effectively Use This Workbook

Welcome to the companion workbook for _Great Ceos Are Lazy_. This workbook is designed to enhance your understanding of the key concepts and core takeaways from the original book. By engaging with the Action Prompts and self-evaluation section, you will have the opportunity to deepen your learning and apply the knowledge gained to your own life.

To make the most of this workbook and maximize its benefits, we recommend following these guidelines:

1. **Begin with the Summary:**
    Start by reading the summary of the original book provided at the beginning of this workbook. This summary will refresh your memory and provide a concise overview of the main ideas, allowing you to establish a solid foundation for further exploration.

2. **Engage with the Chapter Sections:**
    Each chapter in this workbook includes core takeaways and Action Prompts. As you progress through the workbook, take the time to carefully read the core takeaways to reinforce your understanding of the key concepts. These

takeaways act as guideposts, highlighting the most important lessons from each chapter.

After reviewing the core takeaways, delve into the Action Prompts. These questions are designed to encourage deep thinking and self-analysis, enabling you to connect the book's concepts to your own experiences and personal growth journey. Take your time with these questions and be open and honest with yourself as you explore your thoughts and feelings.

3. **Practice Self-Evaluation:**
    The self-evaluation section at the end of this workbook is an opportunity for you to assess your progress and reflect on your overall learning experience. Consider it a moment of self-assessment, allowing you to gauge how effectively you have absorbed and integrated the knowledge from the book.

    The self-evaluation questions are thought-provoking and require you to evaluate your understanding, behavior, and potential changes in perspective. They are designed to help you gauge your personal growth, identify areas for improvement, and set goals for continued development. Use this section as a tool for self-awareness and a catalyst for positive change.

4. **Maintain Consistency:**

To derive the most benefit from this workbook, commit to a consistent and dedicated practice. Set aside regular time in your schedule to engage with the material, answer the reflection questions, and complete the self-evaluation section. Consistency is key to ensuring a meaningful and transformative experience with the workbook.

5.   **Journal and Reflect:**
     Throughout your journey with this workbook, consider keeping a journal or notebook to record your insights, reflections, and any additional thoughts that arise. Writing down your reflections can deepen your understanding, clarify your thoughts, and serve as a valuable resource for future reference.

Remember, this workbook is a companion to the original book, intended to amplify and reinforce your learning experience. Embrace the process of self-discovery, growth, and transformation as you work through each chapter. By engaging fully with the core takeaways, Action Prompts, and self-evaluation section, you will gain a deeper understanding of the material and uncover practical ways to apply it in your own life.

We wish you an enlightening and enriching journey with this workbook. Enjoy the exploration and the rewards it brings!

OVERVIEW

The book _Great CEOs Are Lazy_ by Jim Schleckser is a guide for CEOs and entrepreneurs on how to effectively manage their time and focus on the tasks that truly matter for the growth of their companies. The book is based on insights from thousands of interviews with top CEOs and presents a counterintuitive approach to leadership, arguing that the most effective CEOs are those who are _strategically lazy_.

The book begins with an introduction that sets the stage for the concept of the _lazy_ CEO. It argues that the most productive CEOs are those who focus their efforts on a limited number of tasks that have the most significant impact on their businesses, rather than spreading themselves thin across all tasks.

The book is structured around the concept of the _five hats_ that a CEO should wear: the Learner hat, the Architect hat, the Coach hat, the Engineer hat, and the Player hat. These roles represent the areas where a CEO can make the most significant impact on their organization.

Chapter One, **_Identifying Your Point of Constraint_**, introduces the concept of constraints in a business and argues that the primary mission of a CEO is to identify and remove these constraints. The chapter emphasizes the importance of focusing efforts on the areas that truly make a difference in the business, rather than spreading efforts evenly across all areas.

The book argues that about half of the CEOs know what the big constraint in their organization is, but the other half do not. It emphasizes that constraints should be within the CEO's control and provides an example of a service company that wrongly identified weather conditions as a constraint.

The book then goes on to discuss each of the five hats in detail in the subsequent chapters. The Learner hat is briefly introduced at the end of the summary, indicating that great CEOs realize they don't have all the answers.

CHAPTER ONE:
Identifying Your Point of Constraint

Chapter Summary

In this chapter, Jim Schleckser, emphasizes the importance of identifying and addressing the primary constraints or bottlenecks in a business that hinder its growth and performance. The chapter begins with an analogy of a man looking for his keys under a streetlight, not because he lost them there, but because the light is better. This analogy is used to illustrate how many leaders focus their efforts where they are comfortable, rather than addressing the real problems that may be more challenging or unfamiliar.

The chapter explains that the primary mission of a CEO is to identify and remove constraints in the business, much like unkinking a hose to allow water to flow freely. This concept is based on the Theory of Constraints developed by Eliyahu Goldratt, which suggests that a system is only as strong as its weakest link. Therefore, the most effective way to improve a system is to identify and strengthen its weakest point.

Schleckser criticizes the common practice among CEOs of spreading their time evenly across all tasks and stakeholders, a practice he refers to as *peanut buttering*. Instead, he suggests that CEOs should dedicate a significant portion of their time (between 30 and 50

7

percent) specifically to identifying and addressing the business's main constraint. This focused approach allows the CEO to resolve issues more quickly and effectively, leading to faster progress and growth for the business.

The chapter also emphasizes that CEOs should focus on constraints that are within their control. It is unproductive to blame external factors such as the economy or the weather for a business's problems. Instead, CEOs should focus on internal issues that they can influence and change.

Finally, the chapter introduces the concept of the _five hats_ that CEOs can wear to address constraints: the Learner, the Architect, the Coach, the Engineer, and the Player. Each of these roles represents a different approach to problem-solving and leadership, and the most effective CEOs are those who can switch between these roles as needed.

Key Takeaways

- The primary mission of a CEO is to identify and remove the main constraints in a business.
- The Theory of Constraints suggests that a system is only as strong as its weakest link.
- CEOs should dedicate a significant portion of their time to addressing the business's main constraint.
- CEOs should focus on constraints that are within their control, rather than blaming external factors.
- The most effective CEOs are those who can switch between different roles as needed.
- The *five hats* that CEOs can wear are the Learner, the Architect, the Coach, the Engineer, and the Player.
- CEOs should avoid the practice of *peanut buttering,* or spreading their time evenly across all tasks and stakeholders.
- Focusing on the main constraint allows the CEO to resolve issues more quickly and effectively.
- Half of the CEOs do not know or understand their point of constraint.
- Constraints are controllable and CEOs can make a difference by serving in one of the five high-leverage roles.
- CEOs should not depend on external factors for the success of their business.
- CEOs should be willing to stretch themselves beyond their comfort zones and challenge themselves to tackle tasks that will truly lead to results.

- CEOs should build a strong organization of individuals who would handle all of the work that is not at the point of constraint.
- CEOs should quantitatively measure their objectives to determine if progress is being made.

Action Prompts

1. What do you perceive as the main constraint or bottleneck in your business?

    _____
    _____
    _____
    _____
    _____

2. How much time are you currently dedicating to addressing this constraint?

    _____
    _____
    _____
    _____
    _____

3. Are there any external factors that you have been blaming for your business's problems? How can you shift your focus to internal issues that you can control?

    _____
    _____
    _____
    _____
    _____
    _____

4. Which of the _five hats_ do you tend to wear most often in your role as CEO? Are there any roles that you could stand to embrace more fully?

_____

_____

_____

_____

_____

5. How comfortable are you with stepping out of your comfort zone to address challenging or unfamiliar problems in your business?

_____

_____

_____

_____

_____

6. How can you avoid the practice of _peanut buttering_ and focus more of your time and energy on the tasks that will have the greatest impact on your business's performance?

_____

_____

_____

_____

_____

7.   How can you ensure that your efforts are focused on the main constraint in your business, rather than being spread too thinly across multiple tasks and stakeholders?

_____

_____

_____

_____

_____

8.   How can you measure your progress towards your business's objectives more effectively?

_____

_____

_____

_____

9.   How can you build a stronger organization of individuals who can handle the work that is not at the point of constraint?

_____

_____

_____

_____

_____

10. How can you make a difference in your organization by serving in one of the five high-leverage roles?

_____

_____

_____

_____

_____

_____

Life Changing Exercises

- Conduct a thorough analysis of your business to identify the main constraint or bottleneck.
- Allocate a specific portion of your time each week to addressing this constraint.
- Identify any external factors that you have been blaming for your business's problems and brainstorm ways to shift your focus to internal issues that you can control.
- Reflect on the *five hats* of the CEO and identify ways to incorporate each of these roles into your leadership style.
- Challenge yourself to step out of your comfort zone by tackling a challenging or unfamiliar problem in your business.
- Make a conscious effort to avoid *peanut buttering* by prioritizing tasks based on their impact on your business's performance.
- Regularly review your progress towards your business's objectives and adjust your strategy as needed.
- Build a strong team of individuals who can handle tasks that are not at the point of constraint, freeing you up to focus on the main constraint.
- Practice serving in each of the five high-leverage roles to understand how each one can contribute to your business's success.
- Regularly reassess the main constraint in your business, as it may change over time as your business grows and evolves.

15

CHAPTER TWO: The Learner Hat

Chapter Summary

This chapter is a profound exploration of the importance of continuous learning for CEOs and leaders. The chapter emphasizes that great CEOs realize they don't have all the answers and to keep their company growing, they have to keep learning. This means finding ways to educate oneself both inside and outside the organization. When a CEO puts on the Learner hat, they gain the ability to integrate their prior experience with their new situation and to see over the hill and gauge what's coming next in terms of informing and sparking the kinds of new ideas that will continue to propel their business.

The chapter starts with a quote by Denis Waitley, _Never become so much of an expert that you stop gaining expertise. View life as a continuous learning experience_. It emphasizes that one of the most pivotal roles any CEO can play within an organization is addressing the question, _What's next?_ As an individual dedicated to learning, you embrace the notion of extending your focus to encompass longer timeframes, except when your primary objective is to acquire knowledge that identifies limitations.

The chapter also highlights that CEOs should see everything as a learning opportunity. Whether it's international travel, a conference, a chance meeting with someone outside your industry, or even a failed project, these are all opportunities to learn and expand your thinking. Wearing the Learner hat means you are always on the lookout for opportunities for mastery. While immersed, you should be asking *Why? Why not? What if?*

The chapter warns against the danger of an imbalance where the outflow of ideas is greater than the inflow, which can happen when a leader is doing too much teaching, such as delivering keynotes, participating in conferences, etc. It also cautions against the mindset of *I'm too old to...*, which can limit learning opportunities.

The chapter concludes by emphasizing the importance of modeling learning for your organization, being a thirsty lifelong Learner, embracing various learning techniques, preparing yourself to learn by creating space and quiet in your life, making investing in organizational learning a priority, and using a mastermind group in the form of a CEO peer group, advisory board, or fiduciary board.

Key Takeaways

- Great CEOs realize they don't have all the answers and to keep their company growing, they have to keep learning.
- Embracing the role of a learner involves adopting a broader perspective, unless the purpose of learning is specifically aimed at identifying limitations.
- CEOs should see everything as a learning opportunity.
- Wearing the Learner hat means you are always on the lookout for opportunities for mastery.
- When engrossed in the process of acquiring knowledge, it is crucial to constantly inquire with questions like: _Why? Why not? What if?_
- An imbalance where the outflow of ideas is greater than the inflow can be dangerous.
- The mindset of _I'm too old to..._ can limit learning opportunities.
- CEOs should model learning for their organization.
- CEOs should be thirsty lifelong Learners.
- CEOs should embrace various learning techniques.
- CEOs should prepare themselves to learn by creating space and quiet in their life.
- Investing in organizational learning should be a priority for CEOs.
- CEOs should use a mastermind group in the form of a CEO peer group, advisory board, or fiduciary board.

- The Learner hat is one of the five hats that CEOs should wear, along with the Architect hat, the Coach hat, the Engineer hat, and the Player hat.

Action Prompts

1.   How often do you put on your Learner hat as a CEO or leader?

_____

_____

_____

_____

_____

2.   What new learning opportunities have you explored recently?

_____

_____

_____

_____

_____

3.   How do you balance the outflow and inflow of ideas in your role?

_____

_____

_____

_____

_____

4.   Have you ever limited your learning opportunities with the mindset of _I'm too old to..._? How can you overcome this?

_____

_____

_____

_____

_____

5.   How do you model learning for your organization?

_____

_____

_____

_____

_____

6.   How do you maintain your thirst for lifelong learning?

_____

_____

_____

_____

_____

7.   What learning techniques do you embrace in your role?

_____

_____

_____

_____

_____

8.   How do you create space and quiet in your life for learning?

_____

_____

_____

_____

_____

9. How do you invest in organizational learning?

_____

_____

_____

_____

10. Do you use a mastermind group in the form of a CEO peer group, advisory board, or fiduciary board? If not, how can you start?

_____

_____

_____

_____

_____

Life Changing Exercises

- Identify a new learning opportunity and commit to exploring it.
- Reflect on your balance of outflow and inflow of ideas and make adjustments as necessary.
- Challenge a mindset of *I'm too old to...* by learning something new that you've previously avoided.
- Demonstrate your commitment to learning by sharing a recent learning experience with your team.
- Commit to being a lifelong Learner by setting learning goals for yourself.
- Explore a new learning technique that you haven't used before.
- Schedule regular quiet time for reflection and learning.
- Develop a plan for investing in organizational learning.
- Consider forming a CEO peer group, advisory board, or fiduciary board to support your learning.
- Reflect on your use of the five hats (Learner, Architect, Coach, Engineer, Player) and consider how you can better utilize each one.

CHAPTER THREE: The Architect Act

Chapter Summary

In this chapter, Jim discusses the role of a CEO as an architect, one of the five key roles or _hats_ a CEO should wear. The other roles include the Learner, the Coach, the Engineer, and the Player.

When wearing the Architect hat, a CEO is tasked with improving the existing business model or developing a new business concept and building the elements to support it. This involves planning, strategizing, and plotting. The time invested in this role yields a strong multiplier effect, providing a disproportionate return. The ultimate goal is to construct a superior business model characterized by high margins, a compelling offer, low capital needs, and good recurring revenue. This type of business is easier to grow, operate, and potentially sell.

The Architect hat is often worn when there is a business model issue. The CEO, as an architect, is expected to think long-term about the design of the business, its target audience, and how it will generate revenue. The CEO must face the business model like an architect would when designing any structure, considering the internal integrity and purpose of a great building and a great business.

One of the key skills a CEO wearing the Architect hat can hone is the ability to say no to anything that doesn't add value to the business. The _Don't-Do_ list should be ten times as long as the _To-Do_ list. This approach emphasizes the importance of simplicity and focus in the business model.

Key Takeaways

- The Architect hat is one of the five key roles a CEO should play, alongside the Learner, the Coach, the Engineer, and the Player.
- When wearing the Architect hat, a CEO is involved in improving the existing business model or developing a new one.
- The time invested in this role yields a strong multiplier effect, providing a disproportionate return.
- The objective is to create an exceptional business model that boasts impressive profit margins, an enticing proposition, minimal capital requirements, and a steady stream of recurring revenue.
- The Architect hat is often worn when there is a business model issue.
- The CEO, as an architect, thinks long-term about the design of the business, its target audience, and how it will generate revenue.
- The CEO must face the business model like an architect would when designing any structure.
- The CEO must consider the internal integrity and purpose of a great building and a great business.
- One of the key skills a CEO wearing the Architect hat can hone is the ability to say no to anything that doesn't add value to the business.
- The _Don't-Do_ list should be ten times as long as the _To-Do_ list.
- Simplicity and focus are crucial in the business model.

- The CEO should be ready to change the business model if it doesn't align with the company's long-term vision.
- The CEO should be able to identify opportunities to tackle when wearing the other hats.
- The Architect hat is a high leverage role that can significantly impact the business's direction and success.

Action Prompts

1. How often do you wear your Architect hat as a CEO?

_____

_____

_____

_____

_____

2. What improvements have you made to your existing business model?

_____

_____

_____

_____

3. How do you strategize and plan for your business's future?

_____

_____

_____

_____

4. How do you ensure your business model has high margins, a compelling offer, low capital needs, and good recurring revenue?

_____

_____

_____

_____

_____

_____

5.   How do you handle business model issues?

_____

_____

_____

_____

_____

6.   How do you think long-term about the design of your business, its target audience, and how it will generate revenue?

_____

_____

_____

_____

_____

7.   How do you maintain the internal integrity and purpose of your business?

_____

_____

_____

_____

_____

8. How often do you say no to things that don't add value to your business?

_____

_____

_____

_____

_____

9. How do you maintain simplicity and focus in your business model?

_____

_____

_____

_____

_____

10. How do you identify opportunities to tackle when wearing the other hats?

_____

_____

_____

_____

_____

_____

Life Changing Exercises

- Spend a day each week wearing your Architect hat, focusing on improving your business model.
- Develop a compelling offer for your business that aligns with your business model.
- Regularly review your business model to ensure it has high margins and low capital needs.
- Create a _Don't-Do_ list that is ten times as long as your _To-Do_ list.
- Spend time each week thinking long-term about the design of your business, its target audience, and how it will generate revenue.
- Regularly review and update your business's internal integrity and purpose.
- Practice saying no to things that don't add value to your business.
- Develop a strategy to maintain simplicity and focus in your business model.
- Identify opportunities to tackle when wearing the other hats.
- Regularly review and update your business model to align with your company's long-term vision.

CHAPTER FOUR: The Coach Hat

Chapter Summary

This chapter is a profound exploration of the role of a leader in managing and improving the talent within their organization. The chapter introduces the concept of the Coach Hat, one of the five hats a CEO or leader should wear to effectively guide their organization. The other hats include the Learner, Architect, Engineer, and Player hats.

The Coach Hat is a metaphorical representation of the leader's role in talent management. When wearing the Coach Hat, a leader focuses on employee talent, considering how to acquire it, improve it, and divest themselves of underperforming team members. This hat is particularly relevant when talent is identified as the point of constraint in the organization, that is, the area that is most limiting the organization's growth or performance.

The chapter emphasizes that the Coach Hat is not just about managing talent but also about improving it. The leader, as a coach, should not only identify the strengths and weaknesses of their team members but also work actively to enhance their skills and capabilities. This involves creating an environment that fosters learning and growth, providing constructive feedback, and offering opportunities for professional development.

The chapter also highlights the importance of the Coach Hat in the context of the other hats. For instance, when a leader is in Player mode, they can observe their talent in action, which is crucial for effective coaching. Moreover, the Coach Hat is not worn in isolation but is often used in conjunction with the other hats, depending on the specific needs and constraints of the organization.

In conclusion, the chapter The Coach Hat provides valuable insights into the role of a leader as a coach. It emphasizes the importance of talent management in organizational success and offers practical advice on how leaders can effectively wear the Coach Hat to enhance the talent within their organization.

Key Takeaways

- The Coach Hat represents the leader's role in managing and improving talent within the organization.
- Wearing the Coach Hat involves focusing on how to acquire, improve, and divest underperforming team members.
- The Coach Hat is particularly relevant when talent is the point of constraint in the organization.
- The leader, as a coach, should create an environment that fosters learning and growth.
- Providing constructive feedback and offering opportunities for professional development are key aspects of wearing the Coach Hat.
- The Coach Hat is often used in conjunction with the other hats, depending on the specific needs and constraints of the organization.
- Observing talent in action, such as when in Player mode, is crucial for effective coaching.
- The Coach Hat is not worn in isolation but is part of a broader strategy that includes the Learner, Architect, Engineer, and Player hats.
- The chapter provides practical advice on how leaders can effectively wear the Coach Hat.
- The importance of talent management in organizational success is a key theme of the chapter.
- The Coach Hat is about not just managing talent but also improving it.
- The leader's role as a coach is crucial in enhancing the skills and capabilities of their team members.

- The Coach Hat epitomizes a proactive strategy towards talent management, encompassing dynamic interaction with team members.
- The chapter emphasizes the importance of the Coach Hat in the broader context of organizational leadership.

Action Prompts

1. How do you currently manage and improve talent within your organization?

   _____
   _____
   _____
   _____
   _____
   _____

2. How can you apply the concept of the Coach Hat in your leadership role?

   _____
   _____
   _____
   _____
   _____

3. What strategies do you use to foster learning and growth within your team?

   _____
   _____
   _____
   _____
   _____

4. How do you provide constructive feedback to your team members?

   _____
   _____
   _____

_____

_____

5.   How do you identify the strengths and weaknesses
     of your team members?

_____

_____

_____

_____

_____

6.   How do you balance the use of the Coach Hat with
     the other hats in your leadership role?

_____

_____

_____

_____

_____

7.   How do you identify when talent is the point of
     constraint in your organization?

_____

_____

_____

_____

_____

8.   How can you create more opportunities for professional development within your team?

_____

_____

_____

_____

_____

9.   How do you observe your talent in action, and how does this inform your role as a coach?

_____

_____

_____

_____

_____

10. How can you improve your effectiveness in wearing the Coach Hat?

_____

_____

_____

_____

_____

Life Changing Exercises

- **Conduct a talent audit:** Assess the strengths and weaknesses of your team members and identify areas for improvement.
- **Develop a coaching plan:** Based on your talent audit, develop a plan for how you can improve the skills and capabilities of your team members.
- **Foster a learning environment:** Create an environment that encourages learning and growth, such as by offering professional development opportunities or encouraging knowledge sharing.
- **Practice giving feedback:** Improve your feedback skills by practicing giving constructive feedback to your team members.
- **Wear the Player Hat:** Spend some time in Player mode to observe your talent in action and gain insights for your role as a coach.
- **Balance the hats:** Reflect on how you balance the use of the Coach Hat with the other hats in your leadership role and identify any adjustments you need to make.
- **Identify talent constraints:** Assess whether talent is a point of constraint in your organization and, if so, how you can address this.
- **Implement a talent strategy:** Based on your reflections and assessments, implement a strategy for managing and improving talent within your organization.

- **Reflect on your coaching role:** Regularly reflect on your effectiveness in wearing the Coach Hat and identify any areas for improvement.
- **Continual learning:** Commit to continual learning and improvement in your role as a coach, such as by seeking feedback from your team members or engaging in professional development opportunities.

CHAPTER FIVE: The Engineer Hat

Chapter Summary

This chapter is a comprehensive guide to understanding the role of a CEO as an engineer in an organization. The chapter emphasizes the importance of implementing and improving processes that align with the value proposition of the business, along with the measurement systems to check progress.

The chapter begins by explaining the concept of the Engineer Hat, one of the five hats a CEO should wear, the others being the Learner, Architect, Coach, and Player hats. Each hat represents a different role a CEO plays in an organization. The Engineer Hat is about working on the systems and processes of the organization.

Jim uses the example of Taco Bell to illustrate the power of process improvement. Taco Bell made a small change in their drive-through process, which significantly increased the average order size and thus increased profits. This example demonstrates the kind of impactful process improvement that the Engineer Hat seeks.

Jim also emphasizes the importance of focusing on applications rather than hardware and infrastructure when wearing the Engineer Hat. It suggests that CEOs should think of their IT infrastructure as a public utility, something that should just work when turned on. The

43

value a CEO can add here is not in the technical details but in managing the cost of outsourcing and the service level provided by the outsourced organization.

Towards the end, the chapter explains how CEOs can use the Player Hat for meta-work, i.e., thinking about the process rather than the actual work. This means that while in Player mode, they are also wearing one of the other Lazy CEO hats: Architect, Coach, Engineer, and, primarily, Learner.

Key Takeaways

- The Engineer Hat represents the role of a CEO in implementing and improving processes that align with the business's value proposition.
- The Engineer Hat is one of the five hats a CEO should wear, the others being the Learner, Architect, Coach, and Player hats.
- Process improvement can have a significant impact on the performance of the organization, as illustrated by the Taco Bell example .
- CEOs should focus more on applications and less on hardware and infrastructure when wearing the Engineer Hat.
- CEOs should think of their IT infrastructure as a public utility, something that should just work when turned on.
- The value a CEO can add in the area of IT is not in the technical details but in managing the cost of outsourcing and the service level provided by the outsourced organization.
- CEOs can use the Player Hat for meta-work, i.e., thinking about the process rather than the actual work.
- While in Player mode, CEOs are also wearing one of the other Lazy CEO hats: Architect, Coach, Engineer, and, primarily, Learner.
- The Engineer Hat is about working on the systems and processes of the organization.
- The chapter emphasizes the importance of implementing and improving processes that align

with the value proposition of the business, along with the measurement systems to check progress.

- The Engineer Hat seeks impactful process improvement that lifts the performance of the entire organization.
- The chapter uses the example of Taco Bell to illustrate the power of process improvement.
- The chapter also emphasizes the importance of focusing on applications rather than hardware and infrastructure when wearing the Engineer Hat.
- The chapter explains how CEOs can use the Player Hat for meta-work, i.e., thinking about the process rather than the actual work.

Action Prompts

1. How do you currently approach process improvement in your organization?

_____

_____

_____

_____

_____

2. How can you apply the concept of the Engineer Hat to your role?

_____

_____

_____

_____

3. What systems and processes in your organization could benefit from the Engineer Hat approach?

_____

_____

_____

_____

4. How can you focus more on applications and less on hardware and infrastructure in your role?

_____

_____

_____

_____

_____

_____

5.   How do you manage the cost of outsourcing and the service level provided by outsourced organizations?

_____

_____

_____

_____

_____

6.   How can you use the Player Hat for meta-work in your role?

_____

_____

_____

_____

_____

7.   How can you integrate the other Lazy CEO hats: Architect, Coach, Engineer, and Learner, into your role?

_____

_____

_____

_____

_____

8.   How can you implement and improve processes that align with your business's value proposition?

_____

_____

_____

_____

_____

9.   How can you use measurement systems to check progress in your organization?

_____

_____

_____

_____

10.   How can you seek impactful process improvement that lifts the performance of your entire organization?

_____

_____

_____

_____

_____

Life Changing Exercises

- Identify a process in your organization that could benefit from improvement. Apply the Engineer Hat approach to this process.
- Devote a day to prioritizing applications over hardware and infrastructure and take time to contemplate the shifts in your perspective resulting from this approach.
- Review your outsourcing contracts. Look for ways to manage the cost and improve the service level provided by outsourced organizations.
- Spend a day in Player mode, focusing on meta-work. Reflect on how this changes your perspective.
- Identify a system in your organization that could benefit from the Engineer Hat approach. Apply this approach to the system.
- Develop a measurement system to check progress in your organization. Reflect on how this changes your perspective.
- Identify a way to implement and improve a process that aligns with your business's value proposition. Apply this to the process.
- Spend a day focusing on seeking impactful process improvement. Reflect on how this changes your perspective.
- Identify a way to integrate the other Lazy CEO hats: Architect, Coach, Engineer, and Learner, into your role. Apply this to your role.
- Spend a day focusing on the Engineer Hat. Reflect on how this changes your perspective.

CHAPTER SIX: The Player Hat

Chapter Summary

This chapter delves into the role of a CEO when they put on the _Player Hat,_ one of the five hats a CEO should wear according to Schleckser. The other four hats are the Learner, Architect, Coach, and Engineer hats. The Player Hat represents the CEO's involvement in the company's different functional areas such as sales, marketing, product design, accounting, operations, or any area that aligns with their particular gifts or passions.

The Player Hat allows the CEO to stay in touch with the business and identify opportunities to tackle when wearing the other hats. It's a high leverage role that can be delegated when necessary. However, the challenge lies in knowing when to wear this hat.

When CEOs wear the Player Hat, they are advised to focus on meta-work, which involves thinking about the process rather than the actual work. This means that while in Player mode, they are also wearing one of the other Lazy CEO hats: Architect, Coach, Engineer, and, primarily, Learner. This allows them to gain firsthand knowledge and prevent people from coloring the information they hand over.

Being in Player mode is akin to being in Learner mode, where CEOs can constantly ask valuable questions that help identify and overcome the key constraints in the business from a new perspective. The real opportunity lies in the ability to learn and gather insight into other areas of the business.

However, CEOs should limit their time as a Player. The most gifted Lazy CEOs spend only about 25 percent of their time wearing their Player hats once they are out of start-up mode. They pick one or two go-ahead projects a year in which they identify a constraint on the growth of the business. Spending too much time in Player mode can have serious negative impacts on the company, such as becoming a switchboard operator where everything goes through the CEO, creating a bottleneck.

To get the most out of the Player Hat, CEOs should focus on tasks that have a high impact on the organization, work with a team to assess or coach talent, learn something new from the tasks they are engaged in, and engage in Player mode only around the point of constraint for maximum learning and impact.

Key Takeaways

- The Player Hat represents the CEO's involvement in the company's different functional areas.
- It allows the CEO to stay in touch with the business and identify opportunities.
- The Player Hat is a high leverage role that can be delegated when necessary.
- CEOs should focus on meta-work when wearing the Player Hat.
- Being in Player mode is akin to being in Learner mode.
- The real opportunity lies in the ability to learn and gather insight into other areas of the business.
- CEOs should limit their time as a Player.
- Spending too much time in Player mode can have serious negative impacts on the company.
- CEOs should focus on tasks that have a high impact on the organization when wearing the Player Hat.
- They should work with a team to assess or coach talent.
- They should learn something new from the tasks they are engaged in.
- They should engage in Player mode only around the point of constraint for maximum learning and impact.
- The Player Hat is one of the five hats a CEO should wear, the others being the Learner, Architect, Coach, and Engineer hats.
- The Player Hat allows CEOs to have a clear pathway back into their CEO role.

Action Prompts

1. How often do you wear your Player Hat in your role as a CEO?

    _____

    _____

    _____

    _____

    _____

2. What functional areas of your company do you engage with when wearing your Player Hat?

    _____

    _____

    _____

    _____

    _____

3. How do you ensure that you focus on meta-work when in Player mode?

    _____

    _____

    _____

    _____

    _____

4. What new insights have you gained from wearing your Player Hat?

    _____

    _____

    _____

_____
_____

5. How do you limit your time as a Player to avoid becoming a bottleneck in your company?

_____
_____
_____
_____
_____

6. What high impact tasks do you focus on when wearing your Player Hat?

_____
_____
_____
_____
_____

7. How do you use your time in Player mode to assess or coach your team?

_____
_____
_____
_____
_____
_____

8. What new things have you learned from the tasks you engage in when wearing your Player Hat?

_____

_____

_____

_____

_____

9. How do you ensure that you engage in Player mode only around the point of constraint for maximum learning and impact?

_____

_____

_____

_____

_____

10. How does wearing the Player Hat help you transition back into your CEO role?

_____

_____

_____

_____

_____

Life Changing Exercises

- Identify the functional areas of your company where you can wear your Player Hat.
- Set a limit on the amount of time you spend in Player mode to avoid becoming a bottleneck.
- Identify high impact tasks that you can focus on when wearing your Player Hat.
- Create a plan to work with your team when in Player mode to assess or coach talent.
- Identify new things you can learn from the tasks you engage in when wearing your Player Hat.
- Identify the point of constraint in your company and engage in Player mode around it for maximum learning and impact.
- Reflect on the insights you have gained from wearing your Player Hat and how they can be applied to other areas of your business.
- Practice transitioning from Player mode back into your CEO role.
- Reflect on how wearing the Player Hat has impacted your role as a CEO.
- Create a plan to delegate tasks when necessary to ensure that you are not wearing your Player Hat too often.

Self-Assessment Questions

Reflect on your journey through this workbook. What were the most valuable insights or skills you gained during the process?

_____

_____

_____

_____

_____

Reflect on the obstacles you faced while working on the exercises. Consider the strategies you employed to surmount them and the valuable insights gained from these encounters.

_____

_____

_____

_____

_____

On a scale of 1 to 10, how confident do you feel about applying the knowledge and skills acquired from this workbook in real-life situations? Please explain your rating.

_____

_____

_____

_____

_____

_____

Identify one specific area where you believe you have made significant progress. What steps will you take to continue building upon this progress?

_____

_____

_____

_____

_____

Were there any sections or exercises in the workbook that you found particularly challenging or confusing? If so, which ones and why?

_____

_____

_____

_____

How do you plan to incorporate the concepts and practices from this workbook into your daily life or professional pursuits moving forward?

_____

_____

_____

_____

_____

Made in the USA
Monee, IL
07 August 2023